Morning Light, Quiet Nights

Lynn H. Wyvill

Morning Light, Quiet Nights

Copyright © 2023 by Lynn H. Wyvill

All rights reserved.

This book or any portion thereof may not be reproduced or used in any manner whatsoever without the express written permission of the publisher except for the use of brief quotations in a book review.

Publisher: Lynn H. Wyvill
Fredericksburg, Virginia

Content Editing: Ann F. Hammersmith
Editing, Proofing, and Typesetting: Amber Helt, Rooted in Writing LLC
Cover Design: Melinda Martin, Martin Publishing

ISBN: 978-1-7333545-3-0 (paperback)
ISBN: 978-1-7333545-4-7 (ebook)

I want to sit with the man in you, moon,
  and read stories together.

— "I Love You, Moon"

Contents

Delights
What Will You Think?	3
Applause, Please	4
A Dance A Day	5
Little Beggar	6
The Cloud's Haven	7
The Race	8
The Clouds' Surprise	9
Upside Down	10
Playing with the Wind	11
You'll Miss Me	12
A Squirrel's Desire	13
Little Fists of Gold	14
The Trickster	15
Snow Sprinkles	16
I Love You, Moon	17
Fairy Dance	18

Stillness
Messages of Love	21
Before the Rest of the World Rises	22
Where Peace Resides	23
Sunrise Meditation	24
Late Afternoon at the Beach	25
Blue Heron	26
Whispering Peace	27
A Silent Witness	28
Bringing Joy	29
Holly Babies	30
Three Wishes	31
Listen	32
A Smile	33
Parting	34

Solitude	35
Angels to Comfort Us	36
Like the Turtle	37
The Listening Tree	38

Yearnings

Return of the Loved One	41
Turtle Dreams	42
Cardinal Love	44
Kisses	45
Hurry	46
A Visitor	47
Serenity	48
A Passionate Embrace	49
Sad Sun	50
Cradle of the Sea	51
Memories	52
Optimism	53
What If	54
Amy's Heart	55
They Don't Know	56
A Long Life	57
Fly Away	58
Spring is Coming	59
Happy to be Here	60

Wonders

Lead with Your Heart	63
Wandering and Wondering	64
Crazy	65
Reflection	66
A Sudden Storm	67
The Sky's Surprise	68
Shadows on the Pond	69
Stories	70
Nature's Breath	71
A Welcome Grace	72
Sharing the Flowers	73
Explorers	74

End of Summer	75
Searching	76
Dolphin Commute	77
Busy, Busy	78
Mosquito Love	79
I Wonder	80
My Dream Home	81

Dreams

Caught You	85
Moonlit Ride	86
What Will You Hear?	87
Butterflies in the Breeze	88
The Sea's Broken Heart	89
What I'll Leave Behind	90
In the Night	91
Sleep Like Stars	92
A Night with the Moon	93
After the Storm	94
Prowling the Sky	95
I Am the Moon	96
Can't Wait	97
Tucked In	98
Sweet Words	99
The Night Watchman	100
Little Suns	101
I Prefer the Night	102
Little Dolphin Dreams	103
Acknowledgments	105
Thank You, Reader	107
About the Author	109

Delights

What Will You Think?

Will you think I'm silly
If I lie in the soft grass
And watch clouds float
Across the radiant sky?

Will you think I'm crazy
If I stare at the edge of the woods and
Wait for the doe to appear
With her spotted fawn?

Will you think I'm childish
If I count the rabbits nibbling
Tender grass at the edge
Of the field of corn?

Will you think I'm strange
If I stop to marvel at the
Woolly caterpillar as it
Marches across the rocky trail?

Will you think I'm daft
If I blow the seeds of
A dandelion into the wind
And make a wish?

Applause, Please

A stink bug hurries along
The edge of the rough-hewn farm table.

Eager to impress
He pauses midway, delicately
Balancing like a tightrope walker.

After his dramatic pause
He cautiously tiptoes
To the end of the table
Hesitates
Makes a spectacular turn
And returns to his starting point
Where he looks at me and
Waits for my applause.

A Dance A Day

    Earthworms usually inch along
    Crawling slowly
    But still moving.

    This worm is different
    Leaping off the sidewalk
    Whirling, twirling, landing
    Only to spring up again.

    Why this exuberance?
    "No one needs a reason," he says,
    "To dance at least once a day."

Little Beggar

The squirrel sits on the bottom step
And flashes his adorable
Brown eyes at me.

When he doesn't get what he wants
He comes closer, sits on his hind legs
Folds his paws across his
Furry white chest
And with soulful eyes
Begs for a treat.

He waits for me to weaken.
I wait for him to leave.

Eventually, the little guy tires
Turns to go, but pauses
To look over his shoulder
A final glance, hoping I cave
To his cuteness and give him a treat.

The Cloud's Haven

Today, there were no
Horses galloping
Dogs chasing
Rabbits running
In the pictures the clouds made.

Instead, the sky piled
Mounds of clouds together
High in the heavens
To make a cushion for me.

If I could reach them, I would
Nestle into their softness
Where I'd read a fairy tale
While running my fingers through
The blue ocean of sky.

The Race

The creek races through the woods
Carrying twigs and leaves with it.

They try to keep up
But soon grow dizzy and out of breath.

They stop, clinging to roots and rocks
And tell the creek not to wait for them.

The Clouds' Surprise

>The sun peeked over the clouds
>And giggled at us
>As we ran from the clouds' prank of
>A sudden drenching rain
>That left us soaked and shivering
>Squealing as we dashed for cover.

Upside Down

A family of eight mushrooms
Poses for a picture.

Seven of them stand upright
But the littlest one stands on his head.

He is curious about what
The sky looks like upside down.

He wants to catch as many
Raindrops as he can hold.

His mother and father
Shake their heads and smile.

His brothers and sisters
Pretend not to see him.

He is having so much fun
He doesn't care that he
Is the only one upside down.

Playing with the Wind

The ocean breeze plays with
A plastic cup that bobs up and down
Depending on the wind's mood until

The breeze tires of the game
Drops the cup on the boardwalk
Where it skips ahead of a blond little boy
Determined to catch it.

The breeze and cup like this new game
Waiting until the boy can almost
Grab his prize, before snatching it away
Above his head, out of his reach.

Why is the little boy playing
With a cup when there is
Sand to mold into castles, and
Shells to collect, and
Waves to chase?

You'll Miss Me

You think you can just
Toss me aside
Forget about me?

You think you can erase winter's memories of
The icy wind I blew down your neck and
All the shoveling I made you do?

I'll make it difficult for you to forget the
Wicked cold that crusted ice on the scarf
Wrapped around your face.

You'll long to see snow angels that
The kids make out of the billions
Of snowflakes I'll forge for you.

Oh, yes, you'll miss me
When I'm gone
And the sun's hot breath
Slicks your body with sweat.

A Squirrel's Desire

A squirrel perches on a railing
Staring longingly at a birdfeeder
Just out of his reach.

He focuses on his prize
Calculates the distance
Considers the risk.

Believing the reward
Outweighs the danger
The squirrel swishes his tail
Before launching himself—

Stretching his body to its full length and
Grabbing the feeder with his tiny claws—

Holding on tight, the squirrel
Feasts on a buffet that is his alone.

Little Fists of Gold

The azaleas' white flowers
Open to trumpet spring's arrival.

Their stamens stretch long
Ending in little fists of gold
Sprinkling pollen dust

A gift for bees who come
Close for a hug and a kiss.

The Trickster

In late winter, Mother Nature warms the air.
Daffodils and tulips bloom
Trees burst with pink buds.

The next day, Mother Nature
Turns the air frosty and
Sprinkles snow on spring's green grass.

"What are you doing?" I cry.
"You're confusing the trees
The flowers and me."

"April fools'," Mother Nature giggles.

"It's the twelfth of March," I wail.

"I know, but I couldn't wait," she says.
"Everyone knows I'm a little unpredictable.
It's part of my charm.

"The trees and flowers will be fine.
They really don't mind and
Neither should you."

Snow Sprinkles

Snow sprinkles itself on stiff green pines
Like sugar-dusted gingerbread.

The snow stops to admire its work
And decides much, much more is needed.

The snow spreads a thick coat on the trees
Like buttercream frosting on a cake.

The snow is gone the next day,
The wind has licked it off as a sweet treat.

I Love You, Moon

I want you, moon, to be my beach ball
To play with in the waves of clouds.

I want your craters to be the place
Where I play hide-and-seek.

I want to sit with the man in you, moon,
And read stories together.

I want to throw a party with you
And invite all the stars.

I want to touch your face, moon,
And tell you how much I love you.

Fairy Dance

The wind cradles the honeysuckle
Sings a lullaby to the goldfinches
And rocks forest fairies to sleep.

When night is done
The sun rises
Gently waking all creation.

The forest fairies stretch
Gather in a circle and hold hands.

They sing with the wood thrushes as
The grass tickles their dancing feet.

I watch, not wanting to intrude.
But the forest fairies laugh at my silliness.

They insist we dance and
Sing until night falls

When we curl up on the ground and
The moon sprinkles slumber dust over us.

Stillness

Messages of Love

The ocean creeps onto shore at midnight
Erasing the tracks of gulls and
Pipers that have played there.

When night deepens,
The ocean boldly marches in
To wash away sandcastles.

The sea waits, though,
Until just before dawn
To sweep away messages of love.

Now that the night's and sea's work is done,
A pink ribbon peeks out from the horizon
As the sky awakens and stretches.

The sun rubs sleep from its eyes.
The sand and waves wait for us to return.

Before the Rest of the World Rises

        The dark presses against the windows
        The house settles and creaks
        The moon shines on the grass

        The stars are still

        The birds murmur in their dreams
        The leaves rest in deep sleep.

        I am awake in this sacred silence
        With nothing to disturb my peace.

Where Peace Resides

In the early morning light
In the space between
Sweet dreams and waking

Where the greens are deeper
The birdsong sweeter
The breeze cooler

Peace resides.

Sunrise Meditation

The turtle emerges from her sleep
Pokes her head up from the water
Too shy to let me see the rest of her.

She does not want company
This early in the morning.
Only solitude for her meditation.

I wander away alone
To listen to the yearnings of my heart.

Late Afternoon at the Beach

Hundreds of gulls gather on the beach.
Some nap in the warm afternoon sun
Others watch the waves.

When tired of sitting, they stretch their wings
Circle overhead and return to the soft sand
To nap alongside me.

Salt air skims my body
And ruffles the gulls' feathers.
A mellow drowsiness settles over us.

When afternoon shadows grow long
I stroll off the beach carrying
The sun's glow with me.

Blue Heron

I wanted to see the river
Not disturb the blue heron standing there.

Silently he lifted his magnificent body
Stretched his neck long.

His mighty wings carried him away
To a place to be alone with only
The wind and water as company.

Whispering Peace

A delicate butterfly
Wings painted like the summer sky.

Quietly, I step forward to
Be with her, but she flies
To a distant flower and whispers
"Please go away."

She closes her wings and
Will not open them again.

A Silent Witness

       A hawk sits on a light post
       His broad speckled breast like ermine
       Radiant in the sunlight.

       He waits patiently
       Watchful for the smallest movement.

       What would we discover if we waited
       Silently
       Patiently
       Like the hawk?

Bringing Joy

People gather on the banks of the creek
As I float downstream.
I wonder why they are staring at me.

Just a leisurely Saturday afternoon swim
A perfect current
I fly back to where I started
For another ride.

After the third ride, the creek bank
Is full of people laughing
Taking pictures of me.

I'm happy they're watching me
An ordinary duck
Floating and flying
Just being a duck.

Holly Babies

His shirt hangs on a broken twig,
Shovel and axe lay on the ground.

Shadows dart in and out
Of the trees like ghosts

Leaves rustle, forming words
That are never spoken

Fallen trees rest on the ground
While others lean on the living.

He gently plants his
Holly tree babies in their forever home.

Three Wishes

The clouds formed a magic lamp
A genie popped out and said,
"I'll grant you three wishes."

"Only three," I protested.
"Only three, think carefully," the genie said.

"I wish all people would be mighty listeners
To hear the splash of fish in a lake
The tap of rain on a window.

"I wish all people would be silent sometimes
To hear the voices that are
Shy, afraid, and hurting.

"I wish all of us would be still
To hear our own quiet voice
And that of God's
Deep in our hearts and souls."

Listen

Listen not to hateful words
That separate us.

Listen, instead, for the cry of pain
To be understood and loved.

Listen to hear what wasn't heard before
Listen for what binds us together.

Listen in silence
To the throb of your heart.

Listen in silence to the soundless snow
That brings us peace.

A Smile

On a park bench I sit with
My eyes closed, face turned to the sky.

A chilly spring breeze tries to hug me
But the warm sun won't allow it.

Wind chimes softly ring
Birds joyfully sing.

My eyes open to red rosebuds
Like lips just before they smile.

Parting

Why do the trees shed their leaves
In the chilly autumn air?

Why don't they keep their golds, rich
Like the sun on a late fall afternoon?

Why would they part with those scarlet
Like a cardinal that brightens a gray day?

Why would they drop the fiery orange foliage
That looks like a bonfire on a cold night?

Don't they want their leaves to
Keep them warm in winter?

Maybe, but they know it's time to rest
After painting the leaves.

Solitude

Sometimes the moon welcomes us to
Bask in its radiance.

Sometimes the ocean welcomes us to
Play in its gentle, briny waves.

Sometimes I welcome you to
Share time together.

But

When the moon needs to be alone
It hides behind thick clouds
So we can't guess its secrets.

When the ocean craves solitude
It churns itself into powerful waves
So we can't explore its mysteries.

When I need to be alone
I wander outdoors to think thoughts
I'm not ready to share.

Angels to Comfort Us

In the hush of a winter afternoon
Angels descend on snowflakes
To kiss our faces
And brush away our tears.

Snowflakes blanket the ground
Wrap us in peace so we can hear
God whisper that He loves us.

Like the Turtle

I want the serenity of the turtle
Who submits to the current
And follows wherever the stream leads.

I want the wisdom of the turtle
Who knows when to stop paddling
And rest on a rock in the sun.

I want the bravery of the turtle
Who isn't afraid to venture into
Deep water to swim into the unknown.

I want the pace of the turtle
Who slows down to
Enjoy his world.

The Listening Tree

White petals shaped like tiny ears
Are stuck to the tree's rough bark.

Why does the tree have so many ears
When I only have two?

I asked the tree why
But the tree did not answer.

Maybe it's because there is so much to hear
In a forest if you are very, very quiet.

The flutter of a tiny bird's wings
The scurry of a chipmunk
The brush of one leaf against another
The sigh of cool water as it washes over rocks
The footsteps of a doe and her babies.

Perhaps the old tree has heard
The secrets of lovers
Stretched under its limbs
The laughter of children
Chasing each other
The hum of someone
Watching dragonflies dance
The sighs of someone
Reading a book they will never forget
The cries of someone
Shedding tears with no one to see.

Yearnings

Return of the Loved One

Bid adieu to winter's bitterness.
Welcome spring's sweetness.

Close the fireplace flue.
Open the windows wide.

Sweep away darkness.
Gather in light.

Dance with red robins in the green grass.
Rest among the yellow daffodils.

Splash in puddles of rain.
Run your fingers through moist, fertile soil.

Squeeze spring in a joyful embrace,
A reunion with the one you love.

Turtle Dreams

I was out for a walk Saturday morning
Everything was quiet until
I heard voices and
Felt the ground vibrate.

I look. It's children.
Lots of them.
Running toward me.
The first one to reach me
Squeals, "It's a turtle!"

They form a circle around me and
Bring their faces close to get a better look.
I don't mind, but I am a little shy, so
I pull my head and legs into my shell.

Then I hear them say the most thrilling thing
I've ever heard. They want to
Take me home with them.

My heart is beating so fast.
I'm going on a trip.
I'll have kids to play with.

This will be the most exciting
Thing that's ever happened to me.
Just as they reach for me
I remember that I'll have to
Leave my mom and dad
My brothers and sisters!

Wait, I'm not ready to leave home!

Their teacher saves me. She says
I'm happier here and they shouldn't
Take me home.

The children are disappointed
And I'm a little sad too
To lose my new friends
But I really like it here by the creek.

Cardinal Love

The boy cardinal struts by
Fluffed out in his finest red.

The girl cardinal doesn't notice him.
Crestfallen, he flies to a nearby branch

Where he tries to hide
But she can see him.

She takes two dainty hops
To be closer to him.

But he doesn't see her. Thinking she
Rejected him, the boy cardinal flies off.

She waits, but he doesn't return.
Heartbroken, the girl cardinal flies away.

The boy cardinal comes back
Hoping his love will be there.

He waits. In vain.
This love is not meant to be.

Kisses

Why does the butterfly alight
On a zinnia and close its wings?

Why do we close our eyes
When we kiss?

To love with no distractions
The only ones in the universe.

Hurry

> The sweet sound of rain
> Azaleas dance
> Dogwood blossoms peek out
> Waiting for roses to blush.
>
> Hurry—
>
> The world needs you.

A Visitor

        I'm told a bunny
        Came to the back door
        Looking for me
        But I wasn't here.

        What did he need?
        Did he want to tell me
        He loved me?

Serenity

        I want to live with
        White-blossomed azaleas
        Resting against the cool
        Green leaves of hostas
        Fanned by feathery ferns
        Where serenity resides.

A Passionate Embrace

    Magnificent magenta flowers
    Adorn the crepe myrtles.

    The blooms dazzle but
    It's the tree trunks that fascinate me.

    Their bark cracks and curls, allowing
    Silky cream-colored wood to peek out.

    Their trunks entwine
    In a passionate embrace
    Promising it will always be this way.

Sad Sun

The sun wants to brighten the day
But it can't, not today.

Why is the sun so sad?

Is it lonely because there is no one
To keep it company in the cold?

Is it heartbroken because the
World is unkind?

Cradle of the Sea

        Suspended in the gentle sea
        Luxuriously floating
        Waves hug me
        And ask nothing in return.

Memories

I wish I was sitting by the ocean
But it cannot be
So I watch the blue sky instead.

Warmth radiates
From the flat rock where I lie
As clouds float by with slivers of memories.

The tenderness of his first kiss
The echoing emptiness of homes left behind
The laughter from the stories only we know.

Time to leave
Holding memories close as I
Look forward to tomorrow.

Optimism

The surfer waited for the wave
That never came.

Only swells that teased him
To stand on his board, hoping
One would become a wave.

We are all hopeful surfers waiting
For the thrill of a wave arising
From the smallest ripple of opportunity

Wishing that what we long for
Will eventually come.
Maybe not today or tomorrow
But it will come.

What If

The sea always asks "What if"
And never says
"You can't" or "you mustn't."

The sea grabs my imagination
Stretching it to forever
Where I can think and do anything
Because everything is possible.

What shall I be?
What shall I do?
What makes me happy?
Today?
Tomorrow?

Amy's Heart

      A heart drawn large in the sand
      Surrounds the name "Amy"
      A tender note for all to see.

      A tractor sweeps the sand
      But does not disturb the message.
      Rain does not erase it.
      Nor does the ocean wash it away.

      Mother Nature wants those who pass by
      And Amy to know how deeply she is loved.

They Don't Know

The robin sings
But doesn't know
He soothes my aching heart.

The creek washes over my feet
But doesn't understand
It cools my fevered spirit.

The oak pushes its roots deep
Not realizing
It inspires me to stand strong.

The primrose bursts from the icy ground
But doesn't see
It gives me courage to face the day.

The moon glows
But doesn't know
It encourages me to shine in the darkness.

The sun beams bright
Unaware
That it fills me with hope.

A Long Life

I was born and grew
Into a sturdy tree
Sprouting branches
Searching for life's purpose.

Some limbs barely grew at all
If it was in the wrong direction.
Some dropped to the ground
When they had served their purpose.

Most stretched and grew long
Reaching for sunlight
Touching others
When things felt right.

You may think I'm old
I'm not, just older
Wiser, happier
Contented and at peace
Still reaching for the sun.

Fly Away

A hummingbird darts from
Flower to flower like a
Writer gathering words
Before they fly away.

Spring is Coming

Squirrels leap from tree to tree
Thrilled with the cold.

The river flows quickly
Energized by the frosty air.

Ducks and geese paddle in the pond
Happy there is no one to bother them.

Too cold for the trees, though,
That shake to keep warm.

Too cold for the birds
That fly fast, but don't sing.

Too cold for the pale grass
That looks unwell.

Too cold for the flowers
Hiding until the heat is turned on.

Too cold for me
To leave the warm fire.

But spring will arrive.
It always does.

Happy to be Here

I heard you hum softly at first.
Then a buzz just before
You raised your voice to
A loud insistent whine
To be sure I heard you.

I didn't know where you were until
You gently touched my arm.

You were a beautiful bee
Bright yellow stripes and
Wings almost as big as
Your plump, furry body.

I thought you wanted to escape
My sun-drenched room
To roam free.

When I opened doors and windows
You rested on the floor.
I guess you didn't really
Want to leave me at all.

Wonders

Lead with Your Heart

       A slender earthworm
       Moves slowly and steadily
       Across the paved path

       Stretching her head forward, then
       Pulling her body to catch up
       Pulling, stretching
       Stretching, pulling.

       She leads with her head
       And asks her heart to follow.

       Shouldn't it be the other way around?

Wandering and Wondering

Lush evergreen trees overhead
Leafy ferns at my feet
I wander, wondering
What waits for me in this forest.

Far off the path is a cave
Covered in moss, tucked into
A hill in a clearing of trees.
What lives there?

When the trail turns
Startled wild turkeys dash away
To a hiding place where I can't follow.

Old trees, some barely standing
Others fallen down, their trunks
Knotted, gnarled, twisted into sculptures
That can only be made here.

Crazy

A woodpecker's red head pops up
From the downspout opening.

Why do they think this is the
Perfect place to drill for bugs?

Why do we do crazy things
That bear no fruit?

Reflection

Fog hugs autumn
Coming close to inhale
The earthy fragrance of rain-soaked soil.

The tree has lost a few leaves
But still dances in the wind
In her golden tutu.

Do the trees realize how beautiful
They are when they see
Their reflections in the pond?

A Sudden Storm

Trees in the distance, all gray sticks
Huddle to stay warm
In the dying winter light.

A sudden fierce storm rages
A frigid wind roars
Sturdy evergreens bow
Oak tree limbs thrash
Snow, like thick cream,
Coats the landscape.

Suddenly, the storm gathers up
All the snow and rushes off
Leaving only the lonely cold behind.

The Sky's Surprise

The sky said, "Close your eyes
I have a surprise for you."

When I opened my eyes
Tiny snowflakes fluttered down
On my cheeks and eyelashes.

When I laughed, the sky said,
"Oh, you like that, do you?"
And opened boxes and boxes
Of billions of snowflakes.

The wind said, "Let me play too!"
With the deepest breath ever
It blew out, out, out
Scattering snowflakes everywhere.

The wind grew tired and left
But the snowflakes stayed
Playing under the light of the moon.

Shadows on the Pond

Winter's frosty hands
Grasp my arm and
Lead me to the frozen pond.

Leaves are entombed in the ice
The surface is cracked into
Hundreds of tiny starbursts.

A warm sun and cold air
Hover over March grass that
Is brown, bent, and tangled.

Uprooted trees lie on their sides
A deer nibbles and flees
A bird sings and flies.

I stand with the trees and
Watch shadows play on the pond
Wondering how long winter will stay.

Stories

Rain pelts the house
Wind whips the autumn trees
Leaves fly away like
Fleeting thoughts.

Rain puddles at an old oak's roots
Gathering ideas to become stories
Before the wind blows them away.

Nature's Breath

It breathes hot
It breathes cold
Sometimes it's so tired
It barely breathes at all.

It ruffles flower petals
When it's bored.
It blows leaves
When it wants to play.
It throws sand
When it doesn't get its way.
It rocks the bough
Where baby birds nest.
It rattles windows of the room
Where I watch the storm.

A Welcome Grace

      Tightly closed rosebuds
      On the cusp of life
      Hint at what they will become.

      Slowly, they unfurl
      Birthed into a velvety softness
      Breathing out a subtle fragrance.

      Gradually, the petals age.
      Wrinkled, but still soft
      Their pink turned a tender gold.

      Alive, but transformed
      With so much yet to offer.

Sharing the Flowers

I stand among flowers
Pink, yellow, purple, and orange
Watching the winged ones feast.

A bee carefully cleans
Its antennae before
Sipping the sweet nectar.

A goldfinch clings to the zinnia
As it nibbles its breakfast
Of bountiful seeds.

A butterfly's wings of fire quiver
As its drinks deeply
From the flower's center.

When they are done, I will gather
Some flowers to share but
Always leave enough for my friends
With wings.

Explorers

        Round rolls of baled hay
        Sit atop the slope, waiting.

        But the impatient ones
        Roll down the hill to
        See what the world has to offer.

End of Summer

Summer is fading
Tired flowers drop their petals
It seems not much is left.

The birds, bees, and butterflies know better.
With wings beating fast
They feast on abundant seeds.

I'm fading, too
Wilting in the last days of summer's heat

But I know the coming days will cool
The air will turn crisp
And I will not be able to be still.

Searching

Whitecaps brush the pelicans' breasts
As they search for food.

We fly over an ocean of possibilities
Searching, too, but for what?

Do we look only for the obvious
The easy, the safe?

Do we dive deep
To where we haven't been before?

Will we recognize
What we need when it appears?

Dolphin Commute

Dolphins swim down the beach
Their gleaming backs shimmer
Under the early morning sun.

Their commute is calm
No darting, honking, or speeding.

Where are they going?
What work do they do?

At night, they swim home
Taking their time.

Where do they live?
What do they do when they get there?

It seems a perfect life, so I wonder
Do dolphins ever need to go on vacation?

Busy, Busy

Why do people say
Busy as a bee?

When did you ever see a bee sip sweet nectar
From two flowers at the same time?

Did you ever see a rabbit
Eat while it hops?

Does a squirrel shell an acorn
While it leaps from branch to branch?

Then why do you eat dinner, watch TV
And play on the computer at the same time?

Mosquito Love

Mosquitoes adore my knees
Ankles and the flesh in between.
It must be the juiciest part of me.

They bite and
I scratch the burning red welts
They leave behind.

Where are the barn swallows
To eat these ravenous pests?

I know mosquitoes need to eat
But I don't know
Why it has to be me.

I Wonder

        Clouds like cotton candy
        Tempt me to taste them.
        How sweet are they?

        Clouds like fluffy mattresses
        Beckon me to bounce on them.
        How high could I jump?

        Clouds like stepping stones across a creek
        Invite me to skip from one to another.
        Could I cross the whole sky?

        Clouds like sleepy children
        Beg me for a story. I wonder
        Which one I should tell first?

My Dream Home

I want to climb the highest tree in a forest
And make my home in the canopy of trees.

The pines will shed their needles
To make a soft carpet for me.

Leaves will provide shade
And protect me from the rain.

Birds will sing only of good news.
Squirrels will be my dinner companions.

The wind will cool me in summer.
Snow will decorate the trees in winter.

Owls will wish me good night, sleep well
As God turns on my nightlight—

The moon and stars.

Dreams

Caught You

The moon grinned a guilty smile.
"What have you done?"
Mother Nature asked.

"Nothing," the moon said
With his mouth full
And crumbs on his lips.

Mother Nature said,
"You've gobbled up all the stars!
Why did you do that?
I was saving them for
Everyone who looks up in the sky!"

"I didn't eat all of them,"
The moon said.
"I'm sorry I did it
But you make the best stars.
They're so sweet and buttery."

"Now I need to make more,"
Mother Nature said.
But she didn't mind.
She just laughed when she
Saw her moon's crooked smile
And heard him say,
"I love you, Mama."

Moonlit Ride

Moonlight hovers over me
As I travel an unfamiliar
Winding two-lane country road.

Shadows from trees stretch
Across empty fields.
Cows have long since gone to bed.

Soft light from a solitary lamp
The glow from a television
Peeps out from farmhouse curtains.

But the light inside is no match
For the light of the
Night that is the moon

That follows me no matter
How long I drive or
How many bends are in the road.

What Will You Hear?

In the quiet night, listen to
Your breathing
The owl's call
The gentle rain
The light ruffle of leaves.

In the quiet early morning, listen for
The coo of the mourning dove
The wind's breath
The bees' humming.

In the noisy day, listen for
The splash of the bluebird in a puddle
The beating of your heart.

In rare moments of silence
Listen carefully for
All you've never heard before.

Butterflies in the Breeze

The town awakens and
Busies itself with Saturday's chores.

I sit still and
Watch the morning unfold.

The bright sun warms my back.
A breeze cools the air.

Trees on the mountain ridge
Eagerly wait for autumn's arrival.

Monarch butterflies sail
In the cloudless sky.

In the afternoon, the town
Settles into silence and a nap.

In the shade of an old brick building,
I dream of joining the butterflies.

The Sea's Broken Heart

The sad sea threw itself on the shore.
It wanted to be something else
Something better.

The sad sea was discouraged.
It understood nothing
And nothing understood it.

The sad sea was disappointed.
Some things it wanted but
So much would never be.

Then, one day, before anyone
Awoke, two bright stars
Appeared in the deep blue sky

Bathing the sea with love
To mend its broken heart
So it could go on.

What I'll Leave Behind

        Walk in the lush evergreen woods
        Follow a path—of how long, I can't say
        For what is ahead, I don't know.

        Climb hilly trails that
        Twist and turn, rise and fall
        Before I reach the summit.

        Here my feet will leave the ground
        I'll disappear from earth
        Leaving behind my footprints.

In the Night

The day moved slowly to sunset and its rest
Clouds lingered above the calm ocean
Seagulls bobbed in the water
People strolled on the beach.

When daylight yielded to night
Only the lights from far away ships
The moon and the stars
Shone in the darkness.

The only sound was the ocean that snored
And gently placed, with each breath, frothy
Bubbles full of dreams on the shore.

Sleep Like Stars

My nocturnal roaming
Leads me to the kitchen window.

My wide-open eyes are
Unwilling to close in sleep.

The stars' eyelids flutter
Struggling to stay awake
But sleep won't let them.

I wish I were the stars.

A Night with the Moon

A huge orange sphere, the "Hunter Moon"
Hangs low in the sky.

Ocean waves shimmy in the moonlight
The lights of ships blink in the distance.

The moon spreads a brilliant white carpet
Onto the ocean and
Invites me to join her.

What will we do, moon,
When I come to visit you?

After the Storm

The ocean stuck
Its frothy curled lip out
In a pout from the fog-wrapped sea.

No thunder or lightning
Just relentless rain digging
Deep holes in the sand.

When the wind finally blew away the fog
The clouds dried their eyes
The ocean smiled again.

A hopeful little girl
Hoisted her red and blue kite
High into the soft ocean breeze
Where dreams are made.

Prowling the Sky

A cat crawls out of the night sky
Smoky clouds are his gray fur
His face is in the shadow
Except for the pearly moon
That shines as his eye.

I am silent, but he knows I see him.
He stares, daring me to chase him.

I won't.

He needs to be free to
Prowl the alleys of the sky
Looking for stars.

I Am the Moon

> I am the
> Enchanting
> Seductive
> Mysterious
> Moon.
>
> You can only guess who I am
> When I hide behind a sheer veil of clouds.
>
> You can't know the real me
> When I reveal only half my face.
>
> You can't understand me, even
> When you see my full brilliance.
>
> You want to know all my secrets
> But I will never tell.

Can't Wait

       The bunny stands on its hind legs
       Anxious for the moon's door to open.

       It wants to play hide-and-seek
       Hiding behind clouds so
       The stars can't find him.

Tucked In

The magnificent full moon
Sits on her throne of luxurious clouds
In the velvety blue night sky.

The air sighs contentedly.
Birds sing good night.
Stars sparkle.

The moon watches as
Babies are rocked to sleep
Children are tucked in bed.

Night covers us.
We drift off to sleep.
The moon wishes us sweet dreams.

Sweet Words

It's been too long since I've
Heard the rain's voice
Gently waking me from a deep sleep
In the dark of night.

I lie here, listening
To the whisper of its sweet words
Promising me that it
Will still be here in the morning.

The Night Watchman

As I settle down to sleep
An hour before midnight
An owl, the night watchman, makes
His rounds and tells me,
"All is well with you and me.
Sleep peacefully as I keep
Watch over you."

When I wake in the early, early morn
The owl says,
"All is still well.
Go back to your dreams."

The owl makes his final round at daybreak
Hooting for the last time,
"All is well with you and me.
Now you must wake, and I must sleep."

The moon closes its drowsy eyes as
The sun pops up and nudges
Robins and doves to sing
Luring me away from my bed.

Little Suns

Dandelions like miniature golden suns
Nestle among spring's lush grass.

When they can shine no more
Their flowers become delicate fuzz

Gently puff on their fluffy heads
Make a wish, and it will come true.

I Prefer the Night

The moon was still in the sky
Well after the sun had risen.
It wasn't sleepy.

The moon wanted to see
This daytime that the sun
Always talked about.

The moon saw cars racing
And people rushing.
Life was much busier than
The moon was used to.

The moon loved spending time
With his friend the sun
Seeing so many new things.

The moon liked the day, but
Preferred the night
Where the world was peaceful.

So the moon returned to the night
Happy to be with his friends
The stars in the deep blue sky.

Little Dolphin Dreams

Just after the sun rises
Little dolphins join their friends
Laughing and playing tag
On their way to school.

Do the little dolphins learn
How to swim well there?
How to jump and dive and
Do the tricks that make me laugh?

What do they eat for lunch?
What do they play with friends at recess?
Do they have awesome adventures?
Do they get good grades?

When school is finished
The little dolphins swim home.
They play until their mamas
Call them for dinner.

They do their homework
Kiss everyone goodnight
Then go to bed and
Dream of the day
They will join the ocean's circus.

Acknowledgments

Writing is a solitary pursuit, but I couldn't publish without my team of wonderful supporters. I am fortunate to have two excellent editors. My sister, Ann Hammersmith, read the draft and made many suggestions that helped me polish the draft. Her opinion and insights were invaluable. Amber Helt of Rooted in Writing edited, proofed, and typeset the book. Her experience, organization, attention to detail, and suggestions made my manuscript the book you're holding.

Melinda Martin of Martin Publishing returned for the third time as my cover designer. Her creativity and experience show in the eye-catching covers she produces. She is a joy to work with.

Thanks must go to two people who did not work on this book, but were critical to my development as a writer. Elizabeth Ayres, who was my first creative writing teacher, had an organic approach to teaching writing that freed me to write like I never had before.

My first book editor and coach, Shayla Raquel, patiently guided me through the publication of my first two books. She was the calm, reassuring voice of experience for this new writer. Shayla has moved on to other pursuits, and I miss her.

I owe a huge thanks to my wonderful readers who buy my books and read my newsletter, *A Cup of Tea with Lynn*. I am so grateful for the friendship and support of every one of you.

And, finally, all my thanks and love to my awesome artist husband. He is my number one fan, my first reader, and my best supporter. I'm so happy I have you to share the creative process and my life with.

Thank You, Reader

If you enjoyed *Morning Light, Quiet Nights*, please consider leaving a review on Amazon and/or the platform of your choice. Reviews help indie authors like me find more readers like you.

Join Me for Tea Online

If you'd like to be on the mailing list for Lynn's newsletter, "A Cup of Tea with Lynn" sign up at www.lynnhwyvill.com/subscribe.

Other Books by Lynn H. Wyvill

Nature's Quiet Wisdom

Abundant Strength: A Caregiver's Prayers

Connect with the Author

www.lynnhwyvill.com

www.instagram.com/lynnhwyvill

About the Author

Lynn H. Wyvill is a poet who finds inspiration in spending quiet time in nature. She is mesmerized by ocean waves, soothed by hiking forest trails, and captivated by birds and butterflies playing in flower gardens. Her joy is sharing her love of nature in her poetry. Lynn is the author of two other books of poetry, *Nature's Quiet Wisdom* and *Abundant Strength: A Caregiver's Prayers*. Lynn began writing poetry after careers in radio and television and corporate communications training. She lives in the beautiful state of Virginia with her artist husband.

www.ingramcontent.com/pod-product-compliance
Lightning Source LLC
Chambersburg PA
CBHW031158020426
42333CB00013B/719